How to Come and Go

How to Come and Go

Poems Written By

Jo Barbara Taylor

Chatter House Press
Indianapolis, Indiana

How to Come and Go

For information:

Chatter House Press
7915 S Emerson Ave, Ste B303
Indianapolis, IN 46237

chatterhousepress.com

ISBN: 978-1-937793-37-1

Dedicated to

Richard D. Taylor
the extended Taylor family
and the Coal Creek Girls

Acknowledgements

Appreciation to the editors of the journals in which these poems have appeared, some of them in slightly different forms:

"Lessons" *Bay Leaves*

"Cranberry Crowd" *Remember When*

"Gravel Road" *Flying Island*

"Making the Pledge" *Encore*

"Foreign Country" *Hawthorn Road* and *Southern Poetry Anthology*

"Judy" *Ibbetson Street*

"Reading," "Weeds" *Tipton Poetry Journal*

"Window on the Night," "Hickory Nut Hymn," "Mettle," "Luck" *The Broad River Review*

"Growing Up in a Ford Fairlane" *Boston Literary Magazine* and *Best of Boston Literary Magazine*

"Mapping" *But Does It Rhyme?*

"Mining in the Night Sky" *Grey Sparrow*

"Haiku" *Reckless Writing 2013*

"Flight" *Indiana Voice Journal*

List of Poems

LANDSCAPE

Hewn hands fell woods into prairie,
        land of perpetual flatness.

        Soil black, the plow digs deep,
a disc carves gentle furrows to catch spring seeds.

Gravel road dust strangles a farmhouse,
        and mice make merriment in the walls at night.

        Lilacs purple May,
peonies lounge in roadside ditches.

Knobby fingers draw freehand on jute,
        and ghosts play in the hayloft.

        A red barn anchors the homeplace,
if only in memory.

Mise-en-scène

Brushed blue and amethyst
(shades friendly on a palette)
trick the eye into following
      clouds across the canvas.

Color-caked brushes,
empty paint tubes, turped rags
stipple the ground.

Stroke after stroke
branches in leaf sway
        and sway again.

How lively the paint, how steady
the canvas to host a breeze.

> . . . I set out once again
> On the dark and marvelous way
> From where I began. . . .
> Muriel Rukeyser, *This Place in the Ways*

THREATENED, 1946

I am a man of influence and means.
A doctor. My office in the best building
in town. The Elks and Rotary. Wife,
a son and daughter Susan,

a disappointment. Danny Cicero
and Susan. Two years ago I had to take
her to Lafayette to abort a fetus.
Dr. Sisson owed me a favor.

I said *No more Danny Cicero*.
So she sneaked out. I said *No more sex*.
But here she is pregnant. Again.
Danny Cicero says

No messing with this baby or I'll tell
what you did last time, I'll tell it
all over. I am a man of status
with my hands sutured behind my back.

Passing Stars

...my mother cried; but then there was a star danced,
and under that I was born

W. Shakespeare

In the photograph red hair cascades
like a comet's coma born in fire
over the eyes of my mother.

The night I was born
my mother cried.
Her sorrow, my life.
*But then there was
a star danced.*

On the galactic tide
her star spun
too close to the sun,
and she fell, icy dust.

I am four in the picture,
eyes dark in starlit shadows.
I never saw her before,
never saw her again.

Film is one medium,
the mind another.
I imagine pictures
never taken.

PLAIN BROWN ENVELOPE

like girls very long ago who were innocent
                                   Hayden Carruth

Mother didn't school me in the art of menses.
At thirteen, sheltered from television
tampon ads and titillating drama, I
asked myself how this? how that? when?

I blushed in a darkened health classroom
watching *Girls Growing Up*, then joked
with friends also in the dark.
I wandered feminine products aisles,
wondered how? and when?

In *American Girl* magazine, Modess offered
a free booklet to guide me through the period.
I cut out the form, filled it in, sent it
without telling mother, watched the mailbox,
waited.

Coming of age arrived in a plain brown envelope.
I sneaked it to my room, slipped my finger
under the sealed flap, anxious and
wary.

Sixteen pages between a glossy green cover,
shiny cartoon girl with a pink pony tail
dancing across the front,
enlightened my modest education:

how to prepare for menarche, to use sanitary napkins
and elastic belts, to collect the flow,
wear the cycles of life.

Growing Up In A Ford Fairlane

Billy Bragg rode a BSA motorcycle,
the Golden Flash, a red and gold emblem
fixed on the black tank. Chrome pipes
roared like the MGM lion.

I wasn't allowed to ride behind him,
straddle the black leather seat,
hug him around his back,
but, of course, I did—on back roads
in the next county where no one knew me.
I was sixteen.

We dated in his faded apricot-colored Ford
with tan interior, tortoise shell steering wheel,
a bench seat so a girl could sit close to her guy,
a generous back seat. On the radio
Sonny James sang *Young love, first love...*
Dark spots clawed the felt ceiling
in an unfamiliar constellation.

I had to be home by eleven, plenty of time
to park on country roads in the dark.
He was twenty.

If only Momma and Poppa had known
how much safer I was on the motorcycle.

PRIVATE ROOM

I crawl beneath
heavy branches,
earthy perfume,
purple blossoms,
shutter my eyes
against the day.

Lying on the cool cot
of earthen floor, hidden
in jade leaves
and amethyst petals,
I nibble peanuts
and grape jam.

Under lilac bushes
drops of sunlight dapple
a mosaic on my skin.
A low breeze hums
through the leaves.
An arched bower

of laden limbs protects
me from the heat
of early summer,
prying eyes.
Only there do I feel real.

Eight And On

I am seven in this photograph,
about to be eight in a day or two.
Little girls smile wide,
have nothing to hide,
front teeth missing
waiting for new.

In party dresses and curly tresses,
like angels in candlelight, we circle
cake on a crystal pedestal plate, blink
with the flash.

Years hence, days are ours.
Girls now grown
with experiences all our own,
caring, crying for what is lost
and gained between eight
and eighteen.

Experience takes pictures
through a new lens.
Images develop brides, mothers,
an artist, a teacher, a poet.

Our faces have held smiles
and scowls while posing
for eighteen and on.
At seven or eight, our lives
were pictures still to be taken.

MINING IN THE NIGHT SKY

A satellite skips between quarried stars
in the tourmaline sky. A red eye jet
streams east, trails a horse's tail of mist
over the face of the near moon.

I slip into the mica night, watch
wayward fireflies toss kisses
to the stars, trace the plane,
gray like slate, wish
fly me to Marrakech.
No aeronautical engineer
or astro-physicist, I

understand nothing
except the limits of language
to mine words
that glide on wings,
not sink
like unpolished stone.

Here are fruits, flowers, leaves and branches. . . .
Paul Verlaine, *Romances sans Paroles*

COAL CREEK GIRLS

We began in a yellow schoolhouse with a green metal roof,
  the middle of Geiger's cornfield, Coal Creek curving
   like a young girl's curling sash

Mrs. Parlon taught us to learn:
  the Pledge of Allegiance, the alphabet,
   to walk in line, to fit in

Second grade, we put letters and numbers in place,
  practiced cursive writing. Third, multiplication tables,
   orange-bound books: Ben Franklin, Nancy Hanks

Fourth. Mrs. Luster, white lace blouse and wide skirt,
  fat fingers romped the piano, dancing tunes
   on Friday afternoons, *circle right* and *do-si-do*

Fifth year, fear of sixth grade and Mrs. Foley,
  dour and gray like stone, straight as a Roman column,
   she trained us to be citizen students

We slogged through junior high, stumbled into high school,
  same yellow building, still amid the corn,
   learned grammar, algebra, American history,

to love black dirt, flat land, a small town noon siren
  shared experience,
   friendship that curves through time

MAKING THE PLEDGE

On the first day of first grade,
Mrs. Parlon wrote, "Pledge of Allegiance"
in yellow chalk on a green board.

Does anyone know how to pledge
allegiance? she asked. Unschooled, I sat
on my little chair, waited for instruction.

All stand, look at the flag, put
your right hand over your heart.
She demonstrated patriotic posture.

It didn't work for me, I was putting
my left hand over my right heart.
Gently she rearranged my hands

then turned to the stiff new flag,
stretched above that green board,
clean white, bold in red and blue.

Now repeat: ... one nation
            indivisible
            with liberty
            and justice for all.

When she nodded, I sat, unsure
of what I had learned in that first
lesson on that first day,
but I believed in it and in her.

School Bus, Route 4

Each schoolday morning the straw-colored
bus hurled down the road, lunged into the driveway
(turn-around point), and emitted a sharp,
short beep when Roy's big belly
bounced on the steering wheel.

I marched across the yard, clambered up
two deep steps, walked down the center aisle.
Roy wrenched the gear to clunk the doors shut.
The stop-arm plunked on the side of the bus.

J.T. Watts, the only passenger when I got on,
sat near the front, too young to claim the back.
Next stop, Virgil Butler sauntered to the last row,
slumped in, his sandstone-colored hair sculpted
like a duck's ass, lacquered in preservation.

Then Kathy Campfield, a year younger than I,
got on. We sat together for eleven years,
forty-minute rides to school. Each year
we claimed a seat farther back to show seniority.

The last twenty minutes to school, bus full,
three to a seat, 1st through 12th graders, farm kids.
Twelve years the bus scooted up dust
on gravel roads, ferried me to school
where I learned to travel roads farther afield.

THE BEST PAPER DOLL EVER

My childhood friend Betsy McCall
lived in the pages of a magazine,
dressed for spring, summer, fall
and winter in paper and ink and tabs.

She went to the beach, so cute,
wearing red rubber sandals
and polka-dot bathing suit.
In the September issue Betsy

dressed for the first days of school
in Tartan skirts, cashmere sweaters
ready for autumn days to turn cool.
When it snowed in December,

she donned earmuffs and skates,
blue woolen mittens, etched
curlicues and figure eights
on the shimmering silver icy moon.

The darling, stylish paper girl
wound ribbons round the maypole
in lemon yellow dotted Swiss swirl,
tossed sunshine daisies to the breeze.

Ma knit and sewed my school clothes
to look like Betsy McCall's,
but I never caught the flair, the pose
of the fashionably tabbed paper doll.

MARTHA ANN

After the snow fell, three foot drifts
against fence posts, the temperature sank
to twenty degrees, near zero at night.
For three days. No school.

On Thursday five of us skated on Oppy's Pond
all afternoon, laughing figure-eights, freeze tag,
crack-the-whip. Martha Ann, the best skater,
never fell.

Five o'clock with cold, we wanted hot chocolate.
Martha Ann stayed to glide another time or two.
Mrs. Oppy warmed a pot of cocoa.

Twilight merged into crisp night.
Martha Ann's chocolate grew cold.
We listened for the chink of her skates.

Tom's mother poured the skinned chocolate
back into the cold pot,
phoned Martha's mother.

The men raised her from the pond
midday Friday. We saw the graceful
design etched by her silver blades
near the hole, her figure-eights
turning into infinity.

GENE LAND

went to the picture show
every Saturday afternoon.
His favorite cowboy: Gene Autry.

His legend: when the black-hat riders
hid behind sagebrush to ambush
Autry's posse, he yelled

Watch out! they're waitin' for ya'!

through the inky cavern of the Strand.
Later he moseyed down Main Street,
and the local gang lurked in the alley.

Watch out! they're waitin' for ya'!

they taunted, pretended to hi-ho their hats
and giggle-galloped out of sight.
He grew up waylaid by jeers of boys

aging into men, but always,
he herded the trail, rescued strays
and pathfinders from life's outlaws.

He wore a white hat,
died with his boots on.
His legacy: gentle soul.

GREETINGS

Retard
   the boys yelled from the yellow convertible.
Driving north on Market Street,
they circled the block and shouted it again.

Bobby Bowers, tall Bobby, lifted his grimy
Cardinals cap and waved in greeting.
Then with vacuous eyes and a toothy grin,
the bovine Bobby danced a jig
on the sidewalk softly sing-songing
                              retard, retard, retard

Haiku

Ruth comes to the poetry workshop
curled into the wheelchair, elbows hugging
her knees, fingers folded like origami.

Each week she listens, chin on collarbone,
hair trailing her face. Umber eyes unfocused,
she nods to share without speech.

The health care aide translates
Ruth's thoughts, reads her poems
brief and subtle like haiku.

I glance, though I want to stare
like a child. After weeks
bile scours my throat,

for I cannot overcome my failure,
reduce my sour charity
into seventeen syllables.

Friday Afternoon Shoppers

On Friday afternoon three sisters
walk downtown to shop for trinkets,
spend their coins in Woolworth's.

> *Look at those funny sisters,*
> I blurt.
> *Only two are sisters,*
> my grandmother says,
> *the other one is their mother.*

They shuffle along the sidewalk,
shapeless bodies like yeast dough
swollen before the last punch-down.
They wear shapeless shifts, heavy
ankles spill over the backs
of shabby slippers. Their ages
are lost in vacant faces.

As they amble, they twist
stringy brown hair around
their fingers and chew the ends
like hungry Rapunzels.

> I gawk.
> *It's not polite to stare*
> Grandmother chides.

What else can a child do
when face to face with the oddities
of Friday afternoon?

HOMETOWN KUT & KURL

Doreen Davis seats each bust in the swivel
up-and-down chair of her beauty lair,
swings it back and forth
as she weaves magic in a stylish coiffure.

She stores potions in yellow bottles
and white bowls under the mirror.
She flings a plastic cape in the air,
drapes the torso as if to protect
a marble Aphrodite from rain,
chisels ripples and waves.

White-haired dowagers lean over the salon cistern
each week for a purple rinse. Housewives schedule
quarterly perms, and adolescent girls
seek the edge of a trendy look.

Those who visit on a regular basis are fair
and fare well in Doreen's beauty nook,
but beware,
temper grumbles a spell on the woman
who takes her hair elsewhere and later
must mourn her place in the appointment book.

WHY I SWITCHED TO THE METHODISTS

Rock of Ages
by Augustus M. Toplady (1740-1778)

Rock of ages, cleft for me... Deacon Paul pushed
wooden shutters zigzag, like a snake revealing
the portal to Providence Pond. Jasper jabbed me in the ribs,
leaned down, whispered in my ear, "A drownin'."
I dropped onto the pew, rolled with the music.

Nothing in my hand I bring. Preacher, in somber
black gown, stepped to the window, grazed
the congregation with the flame of grace
in his eyes. He opened a door on his right,
out of sight, for I am short and six rows back.

Thou must save, and thou alone, marching song
for Jess Jeffers as Preacher drew him to *the water
and the blood.* Jess, shiverin' waist up, sang
naked, come to thee for dress. Preacher cuddled
the hymnal like a lace cushion

in his outstretched hand. He grabbed Jess' nape,
pitched him forward *while I draw this fleeting breath.*
Water sloshed. My sluggish church posture sprang
alert—Jasper was right, a drownin'. I hopped up on
the pew. Preacher held Jess down ten minutes, it seemed.

Then he pulled Jess up, cussin' and sputterin',
Could my zeal no respite know.
                              That was the first time
I saw immersion, and I didn't want no part of that
so I found the Methodists, who are content
to sprinkle for mercy. *Let me hide myself in thee.*

Book Report

"*Ride Out The Storm* by Margaret E. Bell,"
the title of Billy Swick's book report
six times in ninth grade. We who caught on
rolled our eyes, giggled every time he stood
at the podium and said the same, lazy old thing.

Mr. Mitchell didn't flinch, just gave Billy Swick
a pass each time. Where was the English
teacher's attention span? Focused on Pam's
short skirt or Susie's recently blossomed bosom.

I read six books that school year,
reported every one, don't remember
anything but the cheek of Billy's scheme.
I never had the verve, the nerve
for such a scam.

JUDY

I'm sorry I made fun
of you. At thirteen, we
all had pimples. Our
teeth were either crooked
or braced. Our bodies were
pudgy trying to find
curves. You were silly then,
unsure and scared of not
belonging. Your teeth
protruded beyond your
profile, lifting your lip
into a constant snivel.
You scraped lesions into
your face, raw with acned
frustration.

We, who thought ourselves
elite, were cruel. We did
not have the courage to
pan you to your face,
but I thought you saw us,
knew we mocked and laughed.
When we thought you were out
of sight, we jutted our
front teeth out and dropped our jaws.

We curled the fingers of
our right hands like claws
on the bridge of our noses,
the fingers of our left
on our chins and pretended
to dig wounds there.

We reveled in our
ruthlessness, unsure and
scared of not belonging.
We thought we were
imitating ugly
but we were just ugly.

Bed Bug Corner

We serpentined the yard riotous with weeds
crowned by Queen Anne's lace to climb
across a rotten wood sill through edgy glass
looking for lost treasure or a corpse in the jilted house.
You first Carl goaded.

Gray floors groaned from years of hibernation.
Fat flies buzzed in lazy resentment. Cobwebs wrapped
themselves around us like ruffles on a petticoat.
Small dust cyclones protested our footsteps,
teased our noses, razzed our throats.
Carl unwrapped Star Burst candies,
littered the floor with primary colors.

We crept, whispered, clutched each other at every turn,
scared of deserted secrets. *Go on* I prompted
at a closed door, anticipating a long forgotten trove
or a cold case discovery. When the door moaned,
we forged a swath through wild weeds,
our bold backs chucking the dilapidated house.
Far enough out to escape danger, we slowed
to a swagger.

Cool Carl said.
The best I agreed.

Freeze Tag

As you walk through the playground overgrown in clover,
a sea of lavender and green echoes *Red Rover*
on the April breeze.
         Crack-the-whip spins kids dizzy
and children swing, one higher than the next.
        (you remember

      and you remember)
sliding on steel polished with wax paper
saved from Superman lunch boxes,
how a teeter-totter squawks around its bar,
singing *Seesaw Margery Daw,*
the tingle of *You're It!*

      (and you notice)
the schoolyard is bruised by nettles and time.
The merry-go-round, once a whirlwind, rots
under a walnut tree, groans with each ghost turn.
Heavy chains tether broken swings to a weak
crosspiece between two misshapen *A's.*
London Bridge Is Falling Down.

The slide, a twisted sluice, no longer scorches bottoms
on a sunshine day. The seesaw squats
cattywampus like an abandoned bomber,
one wing grounded, the other reaching for clouds.
Simon Says: take two giant steps
      (and freeze your playdays in memory)

A warm full moon will rise
out of the mothering dust, out of the dry corn land.
Robert Fitzgerald, *July in Indiana*

How Roots Reach Deep

What stood for love was land,
Midwest soil, black and fertile.
Generations tilled and
cultivated marriage, reared
sturdy stock rooted in the fields.

Later, the land yielded heirs
unable to take root.
They plowed new ground,
rotated crops.

God ain't makin' no more land
Aunt Doris said.
And now uprooted, far away,
I understand the word *heartland*.

FOLLOWING THE ARC

A grinning horse on the merry-go-round
circles its track, the up and down,
the around. A carny organ song
begins and ends, begins again.

The pattern of seasons, harvest to seed
to harvest, the *tk* of seed dropping
in a spring furrow, peace
of corn leaves in summer wind,
crunch of the picker, the sound
of snowflakes falling.

Rotation of crops—corn
in the north field, beans in the south,
wheat across the road, out back
a pasture fallow—the four-spoke wheel
creaks ninety degrees each year.

Hands on a clock follow the arc,
tick night toward day back to night.
The carousel cranks down.

Revolution turns war into peace into war.
The *spt-spt-spt* of guns counts history,
measures the rhythms of life.

Heartland Harvest

The farmer's hand
calloused and hewn
rests on his daughter's
corn-colored hair.
His ax dares
the prairie wind
to blow her away.

Deconstruction

a tornado plays hopscotch
across the land, path uneven
as the bounce of a rubber ball
hungry, it bites roots
from the ground
chews houses
crunches dreams
blurs the landscape
like bits of glass
tumbling in a
kaleidoscope
when the twirl
stops, pieces
jump
into a new
pattern
the old one
forever
lost

Thirteen Ways Of Looking At An Oak Tree
after Wallace Stevens

1
Roots damaged by a bulldozer,
the oak grows stronger, taller each season.

2
Spring tulles the oak
in soft green.

3
A squirrel teeters
on the tottering oak limb
unequal to the tree's treachery.

4
Summer, dense shade
of oak leaves hover
over me.

5
The oak and I share a nightmare:
fire.

6
Oak bark is a yeoman's hands,
gently rough.

7
The oak rains acorns
in autumn.

8
Monk in a brown cassock,
the oak stands barefoot.

9
The oak and the sky are one
on a cloudless day.

10
The winter oak
cannot bear
to lose his rusty leaves.

11
The oak sleeps in a mantle,
dreams his own lofty dreams.

12
The oak lives long enough
to count his blessings
in circles.

13
What do I ask of you, Oak,
a chair, a table, a solid log for
my house or a red leaf
for my book of treasures?

WEEDS

Chicory blooms at 6:23
on a sunrise red morning.
Stick figure stalks capped
with blueberry mops stand
in irregular angles
along country roads,
dot ditches and pastures.
Foliage, edible endive,
graces a garden salad.
Come evening, flowers fade
to tired lilac then close
to sleep in the indigo shadows
of night. Chicory grows strong
from deep roots in summer sun,
witness to the worth of weeds.

Old Spice

The scent of hay baled like fresh cinnamon rolls,
     drifts across fields, along gravel roads,
        through the kitchen window.

In a heavy earthenware bowl yeast gives life
     to flour and water. Butter binds the dough together,
        spice provides personality.

The ripe aroma of Ceylon cinnamon,
     antique and mysterious, crawls
        across the floor and up walls.

In a near field horses neigh for their hay
     as breakfast rolls cool on the counter.
        Who's to say hay isn't sibling with cinnamon?

THERE IS A TIME

Earth has nothing spicier to offer
than this deep-dish field on an autumn day,
serving the perfect decay of summer,
lost leaves on a harvest platter of clay.

Trunks, with deep wrinkled skin of ancient
seamen, raise gnarled hands to wander the sky.
Ready wheat glints through a cornshuck tent,
sings the song of wind rippling through rye.

November chases October into
winter. In this field, soon fallow, sun
gathers fieldfruit, gleans the soil, woos
a cold December, barren as a nun.

The taste of autumn fills an empty cheek
with spice when Earth is lapsing into sleep.

When Persephone Returns To Hades

In September corn turns from green to gold
      and ears sag like an old bachelor's testicles.
           The silk, his spinster lover, dries up.

Tassels waggle like unpinned, brittle brown hair.
      A young girl strips shriveled leaves from the stalks
           to make corn husk dolls and stuff a maiden mattress.

A picker rolls through October.
      The farmer shucks and shells yellow kernels,
           measures bushels, fodders bare cobs to swine.

By November the brown stalks are stubble
      and scratch a withered landscape
           until the plow breaks ground in virgin spring.

FLIGHT

The boy stops his tractor and plow in the bean field,
his hand angles a shade above his eyes.

> The silver hawk slides beneath the lavender
> sky above tufts of blue-tipped clouds

He follows the jet, tracks parallel mists
through blue clouds dappling the sunlight

> like lace doilies on green patchwork.
> It does not dip its wings to greet the boy,

From his singular landed spot, the boy dreams
of his own journey,

> intent on its traced flight,
> on a mission of destination.

Summer Spent

Once I spent a summer
admiring white clouds
against blue sky,
picked raspberries,
watched daisies
dance with roses,
listened to blades of grass
grow
      and whisper
of decapitation.
I sifted clover
for four leaves,
hoping for luck.

Razed

I don't understand why that barn
        is gone. Quonset
roof (corrugated, galvanized)

glint in sun and starlight.
        The farmer held a square dance
under the rounded roof, a christening.

No tamped dirt floor
        (six inches of cement to bear
tractors, balers, combines).

Mouth harp and *do-si-do* drifted
        into an indigo night.
Fiddles whined *allemande left,*

star forward, and rural prosperity
        (in white clover)
sang bucolic ballads. I don't understand

why that barn is gone. Half-moon shelter
        of machine beasts
asleep on raised concrete, patterns

of furrowed life (soil-caked tires,
        loose straw,
errant kernels) where years ago

Saturday night feet promenaded
on the prosperous, pristine barn floor.

Lost Art

At night Jack Frost leapt onto the windowsill,
dipped his brush into ice crystals, painted on glass.
Elm leaves and Spanish fans collided with starbursts,
a collage of temperature and condensation.

Next morning I traced translucent patterns
frozen on panes in the far corner of the kitchen.
Heat from the round coal stove, stoked and blazing,
radiated, and the painting faded.

Jack Frost does not visit houses with central heat
and insulated windows, does not set up his easel
and palette of rime. Once prolific, his masterpieces
are uncatalogued, his art, uncurated.

GRAVEL ROAD

How hard it is to drive in fresh gravel, to keep
the tires straight. Front wheels dig for the weft of the road,
back tires weave a wavy pattern
   that shuttling sound

Dust bloats up as a car trundles down the road,
leaves you cloaked in dirty talcum powder,
croaks a deep cough
      that rasping sound

It's hard to walk in gravel, the clumsy road
stretches ahead, no steady groove, you just slip-slide,
roll with the rocks to balance
         that shifting sound

I know rejiggering gravel, twisting stone under wheels.
The grader guts through grit each week,
the rattle of settling
            that shuffling sound

I remember the hope of a tarvey, black and smooth,
to lay dust on a thirsty day,
pave your way
            that mumbling sound

LANDMARK LOST

The weathered barn,
monument to a farm's survival,
once housed rooting hogs,
Rorschach cows keeping their daily routine,
horses broken to harness.

Yet a scene of death
when the boy fell
from the hayloft long ago.

The red barn,
now razed to some sector in heaven
where barns shelter angels.

FOREIGN COUNTRY

The drooping farmhouse and crumpled barn
stand small among million dollar mansions
cultivated like crops.

The road, once graveled dust
and rock-lined ruts, stretches
blacktop smooth toward upscale
bistros and gourmet supermarkets

where shoppers speak *pesto,*
Perrier, Riesling, baskets hold
Nutella rather than Hershey's,
provincial Brie instead of
American cheddar.

Forty-two acres, an oasis of undevelopment,
speak of a past culture,
the utility of a barn, the muted volleys
like musket fire that identify a Farmall tractor,
sniffs of sassafras, manure and clover.

A bulldozer preys on the
disappearing landscape.
The bushwhacker bullies the farm,
an eyesore to new neighbors.

...and I heard the call
in the old tongue
to come eat
at the long table....
Norbert Krapf , *The Corn Cave*

METTLE

Grandmother sharpened yellow
wooden pencils with a paring knife,
angled each section of the hexagon
turning the pencil in wrinkled fingers,
never manicured.

Granddad stropped his razor on leather.
A strident *waash-waash* pendulumed
on the hide. He trimmed the behavior
of his children, swinging the strap
in work-worn hands.

She beveled butcher knives on a whetstone,
wrapped in an oily rag, used only
for that purpose, steeling the blade,
setting the grind at the proper angle,
gripping with her once-iron fist.

He whetted the scythe for harvest
on the grindstone by the well,
wheel whirled by a treadle setting
off sparks and shrill yelps until he
stilled his hobbled foot.

They whittled a steel life,
honed
to a fine burr.

Facing Day

The barn wears a caul of snow, new fallen,
flake on flake, six inches deep on the ground,
wind-drifted against fence. A stark winter moon
sparks a glist on the snow.

Just before light he shuffles, warm from the bed,
on the cold plank floor. His big toe aches. *Snow.*
He pulls on galoshes and gloves, knitted cap, heavy coat
picks up the shotgun.

Ruckus in the barn last night. Coons, maybe coyotes.
A shiver spills down his rheumatic spine.

Haying the plough horse, milking the Guernseys,
feeding the barn cat. Herd dogs and bloodhounds
yelp for their daily ration. Everyday, snow and shine.

Nothing to account for last night's commotion.
He parks the gun, throws a flake of hay, measures
a rusted coffee can of corn, totes buckets
of fresh water and pails of new milk,
watches the moon fade as sunrise casts amber
over the frosted landscape.

Glad for the caudle that awaits him, he limps
back to the farm house, favoring the sore toe.
The gun's barrel and stock safely broken over his arm,
he collects kindling as he goes.

Hickory Nut Hymn

Along Sugar Creek in the month of October,
wind whispers *alleluia* through the reeds,
wild geese whine an alto chorus
percussed by dropping nuts.

Grandmother walks the creekside
in cotton stockings, old-lady oxfords,
and a ragged wool shirt over her housedress.
She veers to the woods,
kicks pumpkinblood leaves, collects nuts
for brown cake and bread in her apron,
a faded blue calico, old feedsack made useful,
corners clasped in her curled fingers.

She will pick the meat
from the shell's remote caverns,
store in glass jars the delicate flavor
until Thanksgiving, Christmas, next April
for Granddad's birthday kuchen.
Then she will make do with strawberries,
cucumbers, and butter beans while she waits
for October, the turn of the leaves, geese going south
and falling hickory nuts.

CROCKERY

I reach for the heavy bowl, glazed brown like melted
chocolate inside and out: Grandmother's inherited
crock for mixing pancake batter, Jiffy cornbread,
Chef-Boy-R-Dee pizza crust mix---sticky
and hard to rise, or pastry for a one-shell pie.

Which generation's cook dropped the bowl
to break the equilateral triangle in the lip
and a crack, visible from the inside
only, that meanders through
the pottery like Sugar Creek
on an Indiana road map?

The break has not interfered with the strength
of the crock or the flavor of cakes and crusts
stirred in the brown bowl.

Now On Display

The antique pitcher on display,
once shaped by hand in potter's clay
sits dry, purpose lost. Art no doubt,
but nothing pouring from the spout.

Hands spun the wheel with craft and care
fashioned useful homemade ware
kiln-brick baked at fever pitch
handiwork painted to make it rich.

The antique pitcher on display
with Dutch design in blue and gray
held sustenance that fed past lives,
nourished men's tales and poems of wives.

Belly cool to palm, handle strong,
it quenched life's thirst all day long.
No nectar flows now from the trough
designed to draw the fluid off.

The antique pitcher on display,
empty of everyday use today
like a still-life of Monet, no juice to pour,
sits dry with dust, an artful ewer.

HOOKED RUG

Still life fashioned in fabric,
variegated burgundy and currant
frame grinning poppies, dark and bright
like clotting blood, and wildly verdant leaves
within a scalloped bed, oyster white.

The rug gives new life to tired textiles.
The deep reds, granddaddy's
worn out woolen shirts,
the gentle white, an old horse blanket,
the brights from remnants of jackets
and skirts left over from rugs
covering familiar floors.
Long strips, scissor-cut
three-eighths inches wide,
hooked and pulled in a rectangle
of burlap backing, thirty-five
by twenty-four.

Grandmother and her sisters
Aunt Denna and Aunt Mattie drew
the template in indigo ink,
freehand on jute.
Their ancient eyes saw
the design before anyone else.

Wrinkled hands dipped hooks
like ladles into the burlap,
latched wool, and pulled the loops
again and again
until the pattern emerged.
With occasional mumbles
they passed strips back and forth, then
only the rhythm of the hooks.

They ran their fingers over the nap,
checking for consistency
in depth and tension.
When they lay aside the hooks,
they did not behold art,
but found pleasure in the
utility of a rug.

Repeating Pattern

a triolet in b rhyme variation

The nine patch quilt is charted
in the heart and sewn by hand
Blocks arranged, moved, replanned
The nine patch quilt is charted
as legacy to share within the clan
bear witness to life lived on the land
The nine patch quilt is charted
in the heart and sewn by hand

Antique Habit

Anna mends britches and blankets,
knits socks of worn out sweaters,
antique habits learned from her
grandmother's Depression lessons.

> Save lengths of string to tie
> a package or knot together
> to fly a kite.

> Smooth aluminum foil, use
> at least three times for baking,
> seal to store leftovers.

> Wash tin cans to hold hot bacon
> grease for tomorrow's
> seasoning in the frying pan.

> Empty a cotton flour sack to cut
> diapers, dish towels, bandages
> for bones or blood.

In a green generation, Anna abides
by the wisdom of Grandma Edith Anna's
economic scriptures,
                    treasures
the products of her grandmother's
enterprise: a wool hooked rug,
a Christmas tree ornament of twigs
and twine, a crazy quilt on the bed,
the taste of morning eggs cooked
in yesterday's bacon grease.

Lessons

At eight, I loved Aunty Scrap,
her snowdrift hair, her date pudding,
baked umber and rich like antique
walnut, served with a brown sugar
hard sauce that tasted of molasses,
brusque and homespun.

The summer I was fourteen,
Aunty Scrap wore a fusty patina.
I read *Teen Magazine.* She griped,
"A waste of paper." I watched
American Bandstand, she groused,
"You call that dancing? Frog dancing."
I listened to the Tokens.
"No lion can sleep through that
caterwauling," she grumbled.
I thought, "Narrowminded
        old lady."

Later I learned
the parsimony of fourteen,
the recipe for date pudding,
the secret of hard sauce.

WASHDAY NARRATIVE

The clothesline holds stories,
plots that rise and fall, twist in the wind.

Aunty Scrap pins the tales, wringer-wet, heavy
with symbolism, to the rope stretched taut.
Shirts, towels, sheets, take their places in the narrative.

Cousin Carl's sweaty basketball jersey,
last week's game rehashed each washday,
baskets reshot, fouls dismissed.

Aunt Effie's lisle stockings, linen blouses,
and lace-trimmed hankies stained bourbon brown
from dabs of her daily elixir.

Uncle Bart hunts quail and deer in the faded red shirt,
plods fields of cornstalk stubble,
puts meat on the table all winter.

When the rope sags, a pole props up the storyline.
Sun bleaches the bluing out of cotton sheets
and terry towels. High breezes inflate the climax.

Toward evening Aunty Scrap pinches the pins
and folds away the day's tales in denouement.

Window On The Night

The moon reveals red paint
peeling off the barn,
rusted nickel cribs, midnight silos.
I lie on my stomach
hoping for a north breeze
through wire window screen,
observe the sultry night—
a time to watch for phantoms
inhabiting a farm in moon shadows,
to look for the boy who fell
out of the hayloft long ago.

I smell scythed clover and sun
still in prairie soil.
Light spills through leaves,
washes the woodshed raw.
The owl in the maple tree
calls *Ta-woot, Ta-woo*.
Does the boy still play in the loft
when no one is near?

Day-shift animals sing outrage
at the owl's song—soprano meows,
alto moo-snores, a barking tenor,
neigh-snorts on the beat.
An old hog adds bass.
It is a sonata and turns into a dirge
as I imagine the boy swinging
on a rope or riding a bale—
falling, falling

The laborers return to slumber,
and shadows darken the tale.
The barnyard smells like hay
and horses, so earthy, so sweet
I taste it in my throat.
Did he chase a swallow
from its perch, jump bales
of green hay and golden straw?
Did he follow the bird
out the door to catch a breeze,
discover too late he could not fly?

My chin rests on the weathered
windowsill. A breeze shivers
my nose. I swallow
the sore bubble of sorrow.
I see him go into the barn,
climb the ladder unobserved,
unprotected.
He is the moon's specter,
the boy who fell from the hayloft
long before I took up
wakeful watching.

THE BOY

Play time
in October-crisp sun,
the barnyard
my pastime pasture.

I pretend fighter pilot
dipping and soaring.
Trix, the Border Collie,
my noisy co-pilot.

Captain of the *Nautilus,*
submerged
in a murky green sea,
the collie now first mate.

"Ladies and gentlemen…"
I chant, ringmaster
in the big top spotlight,
Trix, a dancing horse.

The red barn, a cave
of cobwebs, smells
of milk and manure.
Nothing to herd, Trix

naps in the sun.
The loft is stacked
with hay and straw,
bales bound with wire

and twine. I build
a fort in Indian Territory,
frame a maze,
lost forever.

The loft door open, I lean
to watch sleeping Trix.
   Falling
  falling
sunshine fills my last breath.

THE MOTHER

Three children, now grown,
have nourished my life.

Like a glutton,
I dined in their lives,
was filled,
but never sated.

Hunger
for the lost one
fed my soul.
Craving

the lost son
sharpened my appetite
for lemon balm
and thyme,

for butter to sauté
sliced grief.
The sharp scent
of sorrow seasoned

each meal,
lingered in my mouth,
though I savored
the flavors

of the growing garden.
I swallowed three
lives whole, more
than I could digest.

How is it then,
I am still malnourished?

CRANBERRY CROWD

Each holiday they wait, anticipate
Great Grandmother's recipe
for cranberry crush, deep red
like mulled Merlot, gelled
into cranberry salad with orange peel
and lemon zest, pecan pieces,
poured into the fluted copper mold.
When cold, knocked onto a flow blue plate.

Now Aunt Barb makes the cranberry
concoction. Young cousins
pass it by. Those who remember
Great Grandmother compliment the dish,
the flavor of nostalgia. Soon enough
that crowd will disappear, the festive table
will look bland and someone will ask
Where's the Cranberry Crowd?

Weaving, Wearing Away

Variegated in color and thickness,
     wheel-spun yarn
battens the warp and weft of family.

Well woven textile
     (unravaged by moth and mildew)
holds tension and the shape of the loom.

When fibers loosen, selvage threads
     break and shed
from the homespun fold.

Holes appear and wind whips,
     (close knit cloth unravels)
chills us to the core.

I will complain, yet praise;
I will bemoan, approve;
And all my sour-sweet days
I will lament and love.
George Herbert, *Bitter Sweet*

WHAT HE BROUGHT INTO THE HOUSE

Granddaddy comes home to the farm on Friday
like one of the Magi, bearing gifts.
He smells of Absorbine and sweaty harness.
He stays the week in the city,
trains trotters at the fairgrounds track, sleeps
downtown in the Claypool Hotel.
He carries a manly leather grip that matches
tan driving boots, wears a brown fedora,
cream kidskin gloves stained with stable,
khaki driving britches, double-seated for the sulky.
He favors a maroon wool shirt, buttoned
down to the wrists and up to the neck.

The suitcase hefts as if full of Indiana limestone.
Open it up! he commands. A week's dirty BVDs,
shirts and socks fill one side, the other hides
tins of sardines and anchovies, a brick of Roquefort,
matches from the hotel, a two-pound box of Fanny May candy,
its white cover embossed with a gold silhouette of Fanny herself
and wrapped in caramel-colors plaid paper, tied with brown string.

At the kitchen table Granddaddy cuts the thin twine
with his pocket knife, passes the paper to Grandmother
for future use. He lifts the lid off small, round mounds
of light and dark chocolate, dappled by pastel tints.
Brushstrokes top each bonbon in a code we do not know.
I choose first, hoping for maple cream in milk chocolate.
Grandmother prefers crunchy toffee. Granddaddy
picks white chocolate knotted with almonds.
We avoid citron fruits, yellow and bitter as flint.
Later he peels back tops of sardine and anchovy cans,
cuts into the bleu Roquefort. Zesty aromas
cling to him.

I did not notice that he smelled
of cigarette smoke, bourbon, and cheap perfume.

On Washington Street

North of Market Street, the Montgomery County Sale Barn,
gray like a dingy winter sky, stands beside the concrete
sidewalk. Livestock is the commodity on Thursday,
and the wooden gavel slaps *sold!* on the podium
like a bolt of thunder in a canyon.

Two blocks down, Crawford Bookstore sells
crisp schoolbooks in September, Dick and Jane
for first graders. Parents and pupils queue
at the door as if the first day of school
were Thanksgiving dinner.

Two blocks farther, Tommy Cummins' Silver Dollar
Tavern serves the stoutest drinks in town
over a red leather bar and sandwiches generous
with pastrami or ham. Granddaddy takes me
there sometimes.

That blue-sky September day at the corner
of Market and Washington, Granddaddy turns
toward the sale barn, Grandmother takes me
to the bookstore. We wait in line to finger
the virgin primers scented with new ink and glue.

With a bag full of arithmetic and reading,
blue-lined tablets for printing,
we step into the sun. She spins
me back inside as if on a playground
merry-go-round.

Grandmother proposes
a chocolate soda in Pauline's Drug Store.
Silver milk shake twirlers wink as we watch
ourselves in the big mirror surrounded
by black and white checkerboard tiles.
She lights an Old Gold,
and smoke curls into the ceiling.

>Years later, I learned why we hustled back
>into the book shop: Granddaddy
>went to the tavern, found his good friend
>Bass Hollis, a bottle of scotch, two hussies.
>The randy men squired the strumpets
>past the bookstore.

After our treat, Grandmother and I meet Granddaddy
in the dusty, smoke-filled sale barn. We spot
his felt fedora near the arena. The gavel
echoes his bid on an angus bull, and I see
that buyers and sellers barter in shades of gray.

Boogie Man

When Uncle Jim boogie-woogied
on the upright piano, ornaments
romped on the Christmas tree,
tinsel shimmied in 4/4 time,
and Granddaddy danced for the kids.
Swinging elbows eight-to-the-bar,
he wiggled his hands, wagged his hips
and dipped into knockknees,
    crisscrossed hands
over knees that met in, fell out.
He cut across the rug,
heels together, toes together,
    heels, toes
        heels, toes
gliding like a reindeer sleigh
'til he danced his pants off!
He shuffled the steps, trousers
draped around his ankles, hoofin'
in his BVD's. Young cousins
in sugarplum pajamas,
squealed with glee.

I, believing myself sophisticated, slunk
into a corner, slouched like a wallflower,
tapped, tapped my foot, rolled my eyes,
forfeited the fun,
misunderstood the romance of the man.

WHAT SKIPS A GENERATION

Dad says he learned horses
from his father.

    how to pitch a stall
    shake up the straw
    wrap the legs and trim a hoof
    to set a bit

    how to sit a sulky
    when to pull back on the lines
    to give 'er her head
    when to pop the whip

    to choose a stud and keep
    a competitive line going

But I learned integrity he says
from my grandfather.

DAD AGING

his shuffled steps
whisper on floorboards,
his hand levitates
for balance

I miss the purposeful stride
on a determined path,
arms swinging
on an updraft of youth

and I wonder
if I will shuffle, search
for balance, what I will miss
of myself

Reading

The white-haired man hunches
over the book, lamplight falls
across his shoulder. His hand,
a crab scratching for the details
he wants. The book, his bible,
an encyclopedia of trotters
and pacers, their lineages
and legacies.

His legacy—a life lived
in stalls, on sulkies punching
a stop watch, hefting harness,
breathing Standardbreds.
Generations of breeding
handed to him,
passed on.

EARLY SPRING LANDSCAPE IN LATE WINTER

At right, the artist sketches in watered burnt umber
half a distant hill, its far side falling off the canvas.
Nearer the eye, cold weather moss
and flakes of last fall's leaves litter a hillock.
Off center, a winter tree, black in its crust,
reaches into a pale sky.

Painted in the gloss of oils, a mound
banked in lemon forsythia, red flowering quince.
Daffodils wink and bow into a fetal curl
under the weight of a stippled snowfall.

Left, stands the thinning skeleton of a barn
and pasture framed by weathered rail fence,
and here the landscapist strokes
a colt caught in a romp, a man once tall
tossing hoar-frosted hay with a pitchfork,
his bones stooped in their own winter.

Stable, 6 A.M.

Sun burnishes the hay,
new-mowed. A breeze shuffles
tasseled corn, promises a hot day.
The cat parades through the barn.
Mare and foal, both bay-brown,
wait for hay, nuzzle
the gnawed wood of the stall gate.
The horseman rubs her nose and ruffles
the colt's short, tuffeted mane.
Day begins in ritual.

LUCK

The horseshoe, rusted,
is tacked by a ten-penny nail
above the barn door.
It is full of luck,
like a woman's legs
curved around a man
in a lucky moment of lust.

A chestnut colt, fenced
in the paddock, threw
the shoe on the track
and hobbled home, four
feet in an uneven gait.

The farrier sweated
a new shoe groomed
to the trotter's hoof.
He hammered it
in the breath of fire,
fixed the bent metal
in the hiss of cold water.

For months the abandoned
shoe hid in brown weeds
beneath the inside fence
of the dirt oval
until rescued as a charm.

For the chestnut, now shod,
the race begins again,
and the symbol of the lust
for luck arcs his steady gait.

SOVEREIGNTY

The pitchfork must hang, tine ends up,
clean, without a scrap of mellow hay
or yellow straw impaled or entwined,
a royal scepter suspended between
two nails hammered into an old oak joist
beside a horseshoe, open for luck.

After mucking the daily dung from each stall,
I slog through weeds to Manure Mountain
and dump moist, steamy horse apples
that attract maggots and gnats.

Barn swallows hover near the mound,
gather thatch and bits of burlap
as they squall and swoop.
They bale nests on rafters and in the loft
high above the upright pitchfork,
simple utensil in the pristine stable.

THE LAST RACE HORSE

italics from
A Song of Simple Love by Alfonso Barrera Valverde

Moment clomps into the trailer and the gate clunks closed
behind her rump. She stomps in the small cavern,
whinnies at the cross ties. The truck crunches gravel in the driveway,
turns right onto the blacktop. She slings her tail over the gate
like a black silk scarf, waves it in the wheel-to-road breeze.
The horseman watches 'til the truck and trailer are beyond his sight.

She is the last race horse. He will not again break a colt to lead.
He will not throw harness over a horse's back, will not
hitch a sulky to the leather and take hold of the reins.
He will not travel the oval track with a stopwatch in his palm
clicking a trotter's speed every quarter mile.

In this moment as he raises his hand, waves goodbye
to the artistry of his life, his fingers seem to disappear
into the *clouds with their caves of silence*.

FOAL

The filly stands less fawn-like
each morning as she sucks the mare's teat.
Broken early to halter and lead,
she frisks the path from barn to pasture.

Each day the foal sheds baby fluff revealing
fine walnut hair. Her short black mane riffles
as she romps. She rolls in the grass,
rubs away the chaff from the stall,
trots beyond the eye of the mother.

Soon she will learn the harness
of discipline and her role on an oval track
just as you and I learned our gaits after we
were weaned from the gentle lead of our mothers.

I came here looking for my life.
Deborah Pope, *Salter Path*

MAPPING

how to get from here to there
　　then farther

paths to explore
　　　　points on the compass rose
　　　　　　the legend of the trek

places you will see and see
　　　　find treasure
　　　　　　or kiss goodbye

how to find the journey's end

How To Come And Go

lay out the route on a pastel map
plan for food and rest, for traffic and weather

pack the suitcase with clean clothes, shoes, shampoo
stack novels in a box, add a notebook to write in

because with any luck the trip will lend itself
to poetry

say *I want to go, but I want to stay*

when the visit nears an end and time travels,
reverse the route and the weather

pack laundry to wash, what's left of the shampoo
stow the unread books and fold the poems away

say goodbye in a wrinkling voice
that cannot find a rhyme

I want to stay, but I want to go

www.ingramcontent.com/pod-product-compliance
Lightning Source LLC
Chambersburg PA
CBHW020949090426
42736CB00010B/1336